Grow and Changing

Written by Teresa Heapy

Contents

Growing and changing 2
Parts of the body 4
Growing taller 6
Eyes change 8
Teeth change 10
Growing stronger 12
Timeline 14

Collins

Growing and changing

You change as you grow.
You begin as a baby –
and you change a lot!

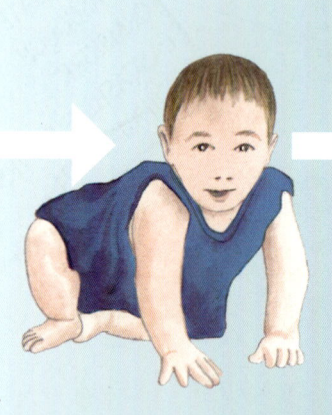

You grow bigger and stronger, and you all look different.

Parts of the body

This baby is six hours old.
He has tiny hands and feet.
His hair and skin are very thin.

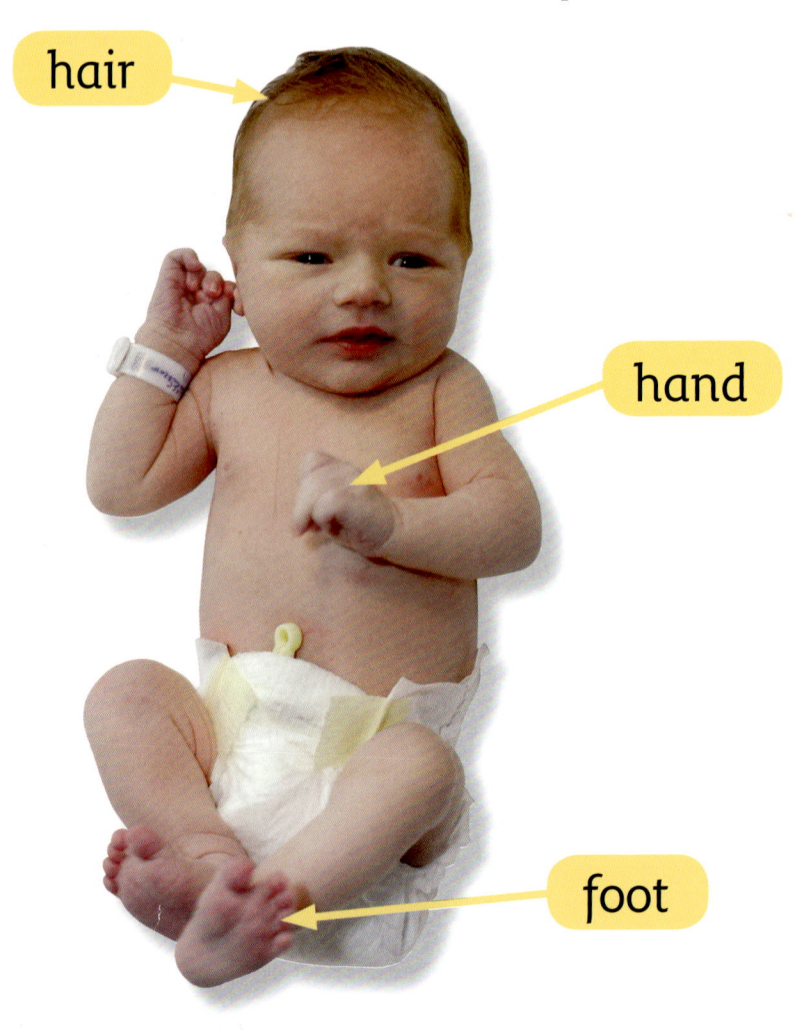

hair

hand

foot

This boy is six years old.
His legs and arms are longer.
His hair is thicker.

hair

arm

leg

Growing taller

You grow taller as you get older. You grow very fast.

120
110
100
90
80
70
60
50
40
30
20
10
0

This newborn baby is 50 centimetres tall.

newborn

This six-year-old girl has grown to 120 centimetres tall.
She will grow taller and taller.

six-year-old

Eyes change

Your eyes often change colour as you grow.

Some newborns' eyes are very dark.

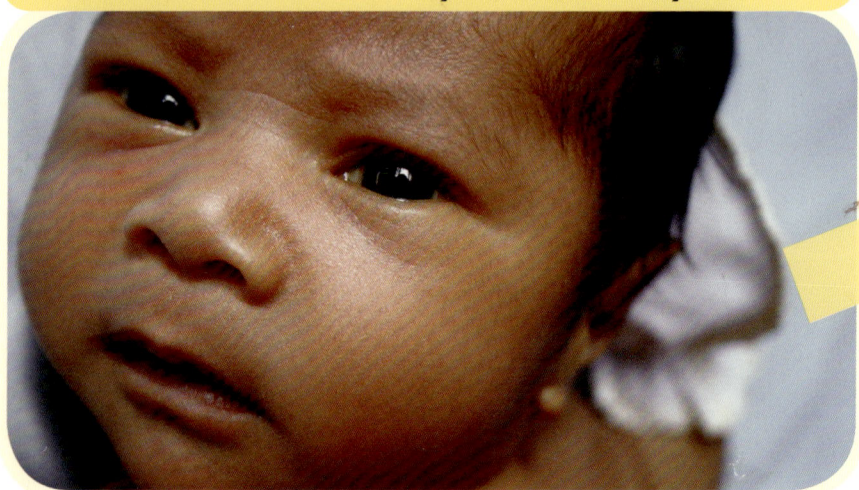

Your eyes usually change colour before you are three.

Eyes may change to brown, blue or green.

Teeth change

You don't have any teeth when you are born.

gums

First teeth are small but strong.

milk teeth

They start to fall out when you are five or six years old. Then adult teeth grow.

adult teeth

Growing stronger

You become stronger as you grow.

Babies can't move much.

Then they crawl.

You can walk, you can jump.
You can do anything!

Then they walk.

Then they can move any way they want!

Timeline

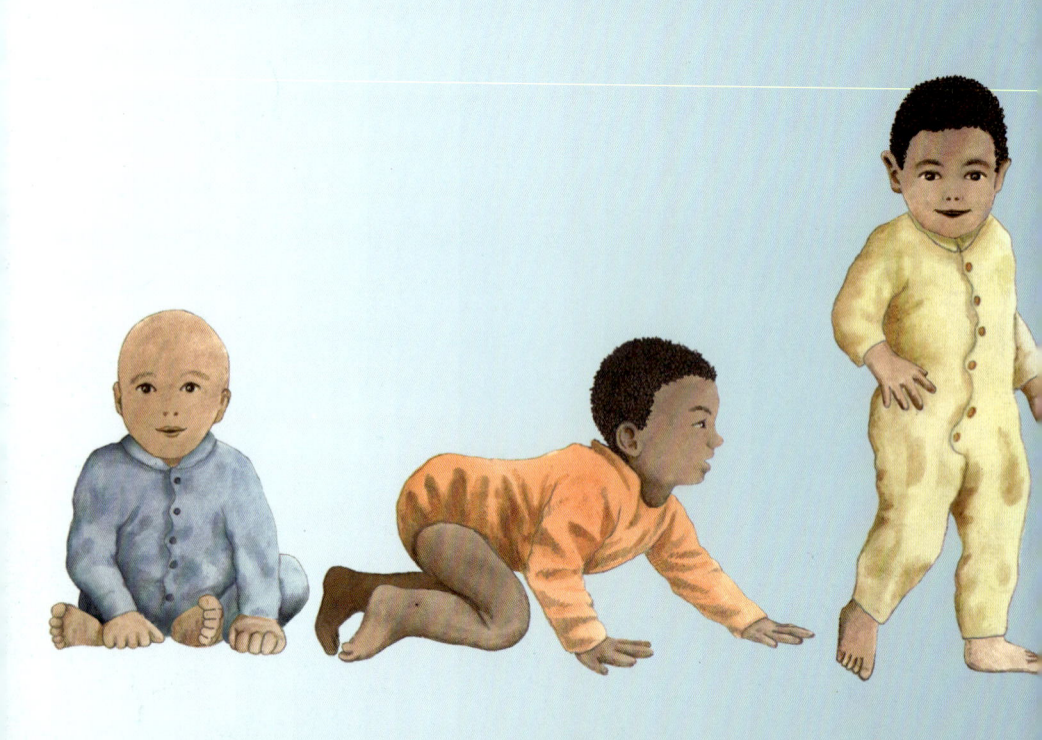

newborn   1 year   2 years

Index

arm   5   foot   4
eyes   8, 9   gums   10

14

3 years   4 years   5 years

hair   4, 5   leg   5
hand   4   skin   4
                   teeth 10, 11

Ideas for reading

Written by Clare Dowdall BA(Ed), MA(Ed)
Lecturer and Primary Literacy Consultant

Learning objectives: take turns to speak, listen to each other's suggestions and talk about what they are going to do; recognise automatically an increasing number of familiar high frequency words; use syntax and context when reading for meaning; find specific information in simple texts; recognise the main elements that shape different texts

Curriculum links: Science: Ourselves

High frequency words: as, your, out, has, very, will, or, have, when, but, then

Interest words: growing, changing, taller, eyes, teeth, stronger, six, hair, years, longer, thicker, newborn, colour

Resources: magnetic letters, photos of children as babies

Word count: 207

Getting started

- Ask children how they have changed since they started going to school, e.g. they are bigger, taller, older, have lost teeth.
- Look at the front cover together. Discuss what the girls are doing and why.
- Read the title and blurb with the children. Ask children to suggest how they will change in the next year.
- Focus on the words *Growing and Changing*. Notice the *-ing* ending. Model how the words *grow* and *change* become *growing* and *changing* using magnetic letters.

Reading and responding

- Look at the contents together. Read them aloud and model how to use them to find specific information.
- Walk through the book and identify the features of this information book, e.g. labels, photographs, information charts, timeline.